BRITISH RAILWAYS STEAMING THROUGH CREWE, DONCASTER, EASTLEIGH AND SWINDON

Compiled by
PETER HANDS

DEFIANT PUBLICATIONS
190 Yoxall Road,
Shirley, Solihull,
West Midlands

Printed on behalf of Richard Netherwood Ltd., by Gorenjski tisk p.o. Slovenia.

CURRENT STEAM PHOTOGRAPH ALBUMS AVAILABLE
FROM DEFIANT PUBLICATIONS

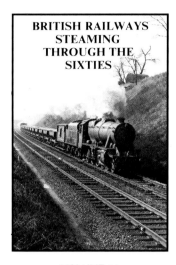

VOLUME 14
A4 size - Hardback. 96 pages
-178 b/w photographs.
£14.95 + £1.50 postage.
ISBN 0 946857 40 7.

VOLUME 15
A4 size - Hardback. 96 pages
-178 b/w photographs.
£16.95 + £1.50 postage.
ISBN 0 946857 52 0.

BRITISH RAILWAYS
STEAMING
THROUGH THE
SIXTIES

IN
PREPARATION

VOLUME 16

VOLUME 1
A4 size - Hardback. 96 pages
-177 b/w photographs.
£14.95 + £1.50 postage.
ISBN 0 946857 41 5.

VOLUME 9
A4 size - Hardback. 96 pages
-177 b/w photographs.
£14.95 + £1.50 postage.
ISBN 0 946857 37 7.

VOLUME 10
A4 size - Hardback. 96 pages
-176 b/w photographs.
£14.95 + £1.50 postage.
ISBN 0 946857 38 5.

VOLUME 11
A4 size - Hardback. 96 pages
-176 b/w photographs.
£16.95 + £1.50 postage.
ISBN 0 946857 48 2.

VOLUME 12
A4 size - Hardback. 96 pages
-176 b/w photographs.
£16.95 + £1.50 postage.
ISBN 0 946857 49 0.

VOLUME 1
A4 size - Hardback. 96 pages
-177 b/w photographs.
£14.95 + £1.50 postage.
ISBN 0 946857 39 3.

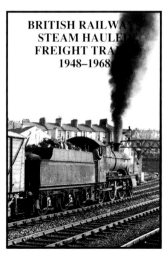

VOLUME 1
A4 size - Hardback. 96 pages
-174 b/w photographs.
£14.95 + £1.50 postage.
ISBN 0 946857 42 3.

VOLUME 1
A4 size - Hardback. 96 pages
-179 b/w photographs.
£15.95 + £1.50 postage.
ISBN 0 946857 43 I.

VOLUME 3
A4 size - Hardback. 96 pages
-183 b/w photographs.
£15.95 + £1.50 postage.
ISBN 0 946857 44 X.

FUTURE STEAM PHOTOGRAPH ALBUMS
AND OTHER TITLES

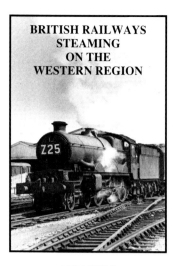

BRITISH RAILWAYS STEAMING ON THE WESTERN REGION

VOLUME 4
A4 size - Hardback. 96 pages
-177 b/w photographs.
£15.95 + £1.50 postage.
ISBN 0 946857 46 6.

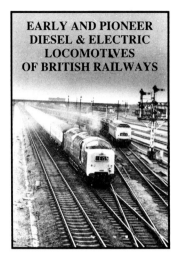

EARLY AND PIONEER DIESEL & ELECTRIC LOCOMOTIVES OF BRITISH RAILWAYS

A4 size - Hardback. 96 pages
-177 b/w photographs.
£15.95 + £1.50 postage.
ISBN 0 946857 45 8.

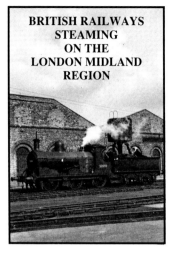

BRITISH RAILWAYS STEAMING ON THE LONDON MIDLAND REGION

VOLUME 4
A4 size - Hardback. 96 pages
-177 b/w photographs.
£15.95 + £1.50 postage.
ISBN 0 946857 47 4.

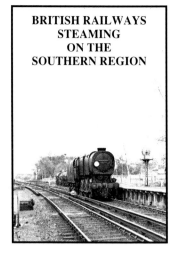

BRITISH RAILWAYS STEAMING ON THE SOUTHERN REGION

VOLUME 3
A4 size - Hardback. 96 pages
-177 b/w photographs.
£17.95 + £1.50 postage.
ISBN 0 946857 54 7.

BRITISH RAILWAYS STEAM HAULED TITLED TRAINS

A4 size - Hardback. 96 pages
-169 b/w photographs.
£16.95 + £1.50 postage.
ISBN 0 946857 51 2.

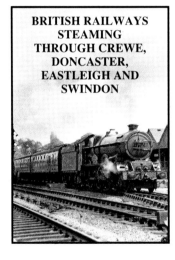

BRITISH RAILWAYS STEAMING THROUGH CREWE, DONCASTER, EASTLEIGH AND SWINDON

A4 size - Hardback. 96 pages
-179 b/w photographs.
£17.95 + £1.50 postage.
ISBN 0 946857 53 9.

BRITISH RAILWAYS STEAMING THROUGH LONDON

IN PREPARATION

BRITISH RAILWAYS STEAMING ON THE EX-LNER LINES

IN PREPARATION

VOLUME 4

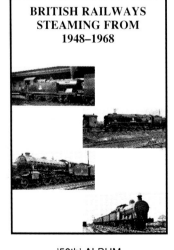

BRITISH RAILWAYS STEAMING FROM 1948–1968

'50th' ALBUM
A4 size - Hardback. 96 pages
-186 b/w photographs.
£16.95 + £1.50 postage.
ISBN 0 946857 50 4.

BRITISH RAILWAYS STEAM HAULED PASSENGER TRAINS IN THE FIFTIES

IN PREPARATION

VOLUME 2

BRITISH RAILWAYS STEAM HAULED PASSENGER TRAINS IN THE SIXTIES

IN PREPARATION

VOLUME 2

It's a dog's life in the FIRE SERVICE
by Peter St. Bernard

COMEDY
269 pages. Cartoons.
£9.95 + £1.00 postage.
ISBN 0 946857 30 X.

ACKNOWLEDGEMENTS

Grateful thanks are extended to the following contributors not only for their use in this book but for their kind patience and long term loan of negatives/photographs whilst this book was being compiled.

T.R.AMOS TAMWORTH	W.BOYDEN BEXHILL	B.W.L.BROOKSBANK MORDEN
N.L.BROWNE ALDERSHOT	R.BUTTERFIELD MIRFIELD	R.S.CARPENTER BIRMINGHAM
TIM FAREBROTHER BOURTON	A.N.H.GLOVER BIRMINGHAM	J.D.GOMERSALL SHEFFIELD
B.K.B.GREEN WARRINGTON	PETER HAY HOVE	R.W.HINTON GLOUCESTER
H.L.HOLLAND ST.CATHERINES, ONTARIO CANADA	F.HORNBY NORTH CHEAM	D.K.JONES MOUNTAIN ASH
R.LEITCH SAWSTON	T.LEWIS **	A.J.PIKE *
N.E.PREEDY HUCCLECOTE	B.RANDS WESTON-SUPER-MARE	P.A.ROWLINGS ALCONBURY
J.SCHATZ LITTLETHORPE	K.L.SEAL ANDOVERSFORD	C.P.STACEY STONY STRATFORD
J.M.TOLSON BIGGLESWADE	D.WEBSTER **	KIT WINDLE LOWER BREDBURY
J.WRAITHMELL MIRFIELD	T.WRIGHT SLOUGH	

*   Courtesy of the Frank Hornby collection.
** Courtesy of the Norman Preedy collection.

Front Cover - A sunny Sunday afternoon depicts a fine Western Region scene. A clean GWR *King* Class 4-6-0 No 6025 *King Henry III*, from 81A Old Oak Common, storms past Swindon Works on 28th May 1961 with a westbound express from Paddington. *King Henry III* was one of the last of the class to be withdrawn, in December 1962. (N.L.Browne)

ISBN 0 946857 53 9

INTRODUCTION

BRITISH RAILWAYS STEAMING THROUGH CREWE, DONCASTER, EASTLEIGH AND SWINDON adds another dimension to the wide variety of photograph albums produced by 'Defiant Publications' over the years.

The author sincerely hopes that the contents of this album will be enjoyed with this trip down memory lane to four of the great towns involved in our railway history.

All four towns have a common denominator, workshop facilities for the construction and repair of steam locomotives, now alas mostly a thing of the past. At their conception thousands of men were employed within them and vast 'railway estates' were built to accommodate them and their families and skills were handed down from father to son.

Although these towns belonged to different railway companies all involved were dedicated to the great cause that was steam and within the pages of this book we can relive those days in part.

In this book and in all of the photograph albums, wherever possible, no famous names will be found nor will photographs which have been published before be used. The photographs chosen have been carefully selected to give a mixture of action, shed, workshop and scrapyard scenes.

The majority of photographs used in BRITISH RAILWAYS STEAMING THROUGH CREWE, DONCASTER, EASTLEIGH AND SWINDON have been contributed by readers of Peter Hands' series of booklets entitled "What Happened to Steam" & "BR Steam Shed Allocations" and from readers of the earlier "BR Steaming Through The Sixties" albums. In normal circumstances these may have been hidden from the pulic eye forever.

The continuation of these photograph albums depends upon *you* the reader. If you wish to join my mailing list for future albums and/or feel you have suitable material of BR steam locomotives between 1948-1968 and wish to contribute them towards future albums, please contact

Tel. No.   Peter Hands,
0121 745-8421   190 Yoxall Road,
         Shirley, Solihull,
         West Midlands B90 3RN

CONTENTS

CHAPTER ONE - CREWE

1) A sentinel-looking floodlight tower reaches to the skies as it overlooks the depot at 5B Crewe (South) on 8th April 1962. Early spring sunshine highlights an unidentified LMS Class 3F 'Jinty' 0-6-0T, LMS Class 5 4-6-0 No 45244, a visitor from 12B Carlisle (Upperby), and locally based LMS Class 6P5F 2-6-0 No 42940. During the fifties the sheds at both Crewe (North) and Crewe (South) boasted a combined allocation of around 250 locomotives. (N.L.Browne)

2) At the height of the summer service in the fifties between 400 and 500 trains were dealt with on a Saturday at Crewe's then 16 platforms. On 6th April 1952 we can just make out the gloomy confines of the station as LMS Class 4 2-6-4T No 42174, of 17A Derby, stands in bright sunlight, light engine. No 42174 is carrying a local passenger headcode and sports the logo of its new owner on the side water tanks. (B.K.B.Green)

3) In the twilight of its illustrious career handling top-link expresses on the West Coast Main Line, LMS *Coronation* Class 4-6-2 No 46240 *City of Coventry*, from 1A Willesden, steams majestically into the southern end of Crewe station with the down *Lakes Express* on 29th August 1964, a matter of days before being transferred to its final home at 5A Crewe (North) Once a long-standing inmate at 1B Camden, No 46240 was withdrawn in October 1964. (Kit Windle)

4) Apart from the named LMS classes of 4-6-0's and 4-6-2's all types of steam locomotives were employed on passenger and freight traffic at Crewe, especially during the summer services. Carrying the train reporting number W660, 84G Shrewsbury based BR Class 5 4-6-0 No 73128 stands on a middle road at Crewe as it awaits a change of footplate crew on a summer's day in June 1957. It was transferred to 26F Patricroft in September 1958. (N.E.Preedy)

5) Like the above engine LMS Class 5 4-6-0 No 44687 (8M Southport) was fitted with Caprotti valve gear which did little to enhance their looks. On an unknown day in 1965 No 44687 sets off southbound with a local passenger service. Once of 9A Longsight (Manchester), 5B Crewe (South) and 6G Llandudno Junction, No 44687 was taken out of revenue earning service from 8M Southport in January 1966 and later cut up at Cashmores, Great Bridge. (D.K.Jones)

6) The 'racing ground' immediately to the south of Crewe was a popular venue for spotters and photographers alike when steam was 'king'. The photographer and a young lad occupy precarious positions by the up main as 5A Crewe (North) based LMS *Jubilee* Class 4-6-0 No 45647 *Sturdee* blackens the skyline as it storms southwards with a Liverpool to Bletchley excursion (1097) in August 1962, some four years plus away from withdrawal. (Kit Windle)

7) To complement the ranks of LMS Pacifics a number of BR *Britannia* Class 4-6-2's were also employed on expresses on the West Coast Main Line from depots like Aston, Longsight (Manchester), Polmadie (Glasgow) and Willesden. Looking in pristine condition No 70031 *Byron* (21D Aston) gently lifts its safety valves at Crewe in August 1962 whilst being employed on a lengthy Glasgow (Central) to London (Euston) relief express. (Kit Windle)

8) It is only when an excellent panoramic photograph is utilised that one can appreciate the 'clutter' associated with overhead electrification with the myriad of catenary posts and wires spoiling the view. Despite the 'modernisation' LMS *Coronation* Class 4-6-2 No 46244 *King George VI*, from 12A Carlisle (Kingmoor), steams defiantly into Crewe beneath the 'wires' from the North Wales direction with the up *Welshman* express in April 1962. (Kit Windle)

9) The evening shadows are cast at the north end of Crewe station in July 1962 as some gentlemen go about their business in the background. In the foreground ('bulled-up') is 2A Rugby based LMS *Jubilee* Class 4-6-0 No 45733 *Novelty* at the head of a rake of stock. During the latter years of its working life *Novelty* was also allocated to the sheds at 3B Bushbury, 5A Crewe (North), 8A Edge Hill, 6G Llandudno Junction, 1B Camden and 1A Willesden. (Kit Windle)

10) Departing from Crewe (southbound) trains passed the once extensive sidings at Basford Hall and this photograph is taken well before the arrival of the overhead wires. LMS *Jubilee* Class 4-6-0 No 45633 *Aden*, of 10B Blackpool, accelerates towards the camera and on to Stafford with a Workington to Euston express on 10th June 1956. Drafted to 24L Carnforth in September 1961, No 45633 later served from 17A Derby and 8B Warrington. (T.Lewis)

11) 1964 was really the last year that a large variety of steam locomotive types were to be seen at Crewe for by then the ranks of the LMS named 4-6-0's and 4-6-2's were decimated. One of the survivors, *Royal Scot* Class 4-6-0 No 46155 *The Lancer*, a local steed from 5A, lets off steam from its cylinder cocks as it waits to take forward the northbound *Lakes Express* after it arrives from London in August 1964, four months prior to withdrawal.

12) A trio of immaculate locomotives fresh from overhaul at the nearby workshops thread their way through Crewe station as they reverse towards the shed at Crewe (South) on an unknown day in July 1962. At the forefront is 27C Southport allocated LMS Class 5 4-6-0 No 45218, behind which is a sister engine and an LMS *Jubilee* Class 4-6-0. No 45218 was drafted to 12C Carlisle (Canal) in January 1963 and it ended its career in April 1966. (N.E.Preedy)

13) We take our leave of Crewe station with this excellent shot taken - circa 1957. On a centre road LMS Unrebuilt *Patriot* Class 4-6-0 No 45510 (1A Willesden) steams towards the camera and heads for the shed at Crewe (South) light engine. Lurking in the shadows in the left of the frame is LMS *Royal Scot* Class 4-6-0 No 46167 *The Hertfordshire Regiment*, a local engine from 5A, which is ready to depart with a Euston bound 'extra'. (T.Lewis)

14) We now concentrate on the 'premier' depot at Crewe, the North (5A), once owned by the London and North Western Railway. The shed consisted of two straight structures and a half-covered semi-roundhouse. A member of the footplate crew of LMS *Royal Scot* Class 4-6-0 No 46128 *The Lovat Scouts*, a local engine, alights from his steed as it poses on the turntable outside the 'roundhouse' on an unknown date in the mid-fifties. (R.W.Hinton)

15) Crewe (North) was famous for its allocation of LMS *Patriot*, *Jubilee*, *Royal Scot*, *Princess*, *Coronation* and later *Britannia* locomotives, but it also housed a number of lesser types, including LMS Class 2P 4-4-0 No 40659 which is captured by the camera in the open on a sunny 12th August 1951. Transferred to 1C Watford in November 1959, No 40659 was destined to survive in service there until withdrawal in August 1961. (B.K.B.Green)

16) As well as having its own allocation Crewe (North) also played host to locomotives fresh from overhaul at the nearby workshops. Looking resplendent in a fresh coat of paint on 11th May 1952 is LMS Ivatt Class 2 2-6-2T No 41310 which is standing near to an unidentified LMS Class 5 4-6-0. Between the two locomotives is a row of terraced dwellings which in common with all railway towns were built to house the railway workforces. (B.K.B.Green)

17) The 29th September 1963 was the occasion of a Warwickshire Railway Society special hauled from Birmingham (Snow Hill) to Crewe via Shrewsbury by a spruced-up LMS *Coronation* Class 4-6-2 No 46245 *City of London* (1A Willesden). It is seen here near to the coaling plant after arriving at Crewe in the company of LMS *Royal Scot* Class 4-6-0 No 46155 *The Lancer*, a local inhabitant of 5A. Both engines were to become a memory by the end of 1964. (D.K.Jones)

18) BR *Britannia* Class 4-6-2 No 70048 *The Territorial Army 1908-1958* never carried a name until 1958 and is seen in the open at Crewe (North) in a begrimed state on 30th November 1962. The shedplate, 1A, tells us that it is allocated to Willesden shed, but this was for only a brief period of time, from October to December 1962. Once of 6J Holyhead, No 70048 was based at a host of motive power depots before withdrawal in May 1967. (R.W.Hinton)

19) Looking fresh from overhaul 66A Polmadie (Glasgow) LMS *Coronation* Class 4-6-2 No 46231 *Duchess of Atholl* is steamed and ready for the road in the yard at 5A in the company of an unidentified LMS *Jubilee* Class 4-6-0 and English Electric Type 4 Diesel No D329 on 28th September 1961. Condemned from Polmadie in December 1962 *Duchess of Atholl* was stored at 66E Carstairs for almost twelve months before being scrapped at Crewe Works. (N.L.Browne)

20) The LMS Ivatt Class 4 2-6-0's were a modern design (1947) and were easily recognisable with their extremely high running plates, making them easy to maintain. In a virtually brand new condition No 43025 is noted in fine fettle in the yard at Crewe (North) on 6th February 1949. Some members of the class, like No 43025, were originally equipped with double chimneys, but all later reverted to more conventional single ones. (A.N.H.Glover)

21) Eighteen examples of the LMS *Patriot* Class 4-6-0's were rebuilt and were almost identical in looks to the *Royal Scot* Class of 4-6-0's. The unrebuilt versions were rendered extinct in November 1962 whereas some of the rebuilt engines survived into 1965. On 8th April 1962 No 45523 *Bangor* is a visitor to 5A from 1A Willesden. *Bangor* remained at Willesden shed until condemnation in January 1964, after which it was cut up at Crewe Works. (N.L.Browne)

22) For many years BR Class 2 2-6-0 No 78007 was an inmate at 89C Machynlleth on the Western Region. Surplus to requirements at 89C, No 78007 was transferred to Crewe (North) in June 1963 where it is noted two months later on 17th August. In June of the following year it was despatched 'down the road' to Crewe (South) where it remained until March 1965. During its last two years of life it was based at 9G Gorton, 9E Trafford Park and 9K Bolton. (N.E.Preedy)

23) The second member of the LMS *Royal Scot* Class 4-6-0's No 46101 *Royal Scots Grey* is ready for its next turn in April 1962 on which date it was allocated to 6G Llandudno Junction. Although an extremely busy shed the yard at Crewe (North) is very tidy and free of the usual 'bric-a-brac' associated with steam depots. Rendered redundant from the West Coast Main Line in January 1963, No 46101 was drafted to 16D Annesley. (J.Wraithmell)

24) By the time this photograph was taken Crewe (North) shed had been closed to steam for some two months with its remaining stock either being transferred away or condemned. All is still and quiet within the half-roundhouse on 15th August 1965. Noted in store, minus chimney, is LMS Ivatt Class 4 2-6-0 No 43026, officially allocated to Crewe (South). Despite being stored, No 43026 was not taken out of revenue earning service until September 1966. (F.Hornby)

25) The coupling rods and paintwork glisten and glimmer in bright sunshine at Crewe (North) on an unknown date in 1949 as LMS Ivatt Class 2 2-6-2T No 41229 poses for the camera after emerging from Crewe Works. No 41229 was based at 5A from new until just prior to the closure of the shed. After a very brief spell at Crewe (South) it moved on to pastures new at 5D Stoke. Its last home base was at 12B Carlisle (Upperby). (R.S.Carpenter)

26) Always second to the North shed in terms of importance the South shed (5B) was destined to outlive the former by some two years or so. Although primarily a freight orientated depot it often housed named passenger engines such as LMS *Jubilee* Class 4-6-0 No 45613 *Kenya* seen here basking in bright winter sunshine outside the running shed on 19th February 1961. *Kenya* ended its days at 12A Carlisle (Kingmoor) withdrawn in September 1964. (A.N.H.Glover)

27) As modernisation began to bite Crewe (South) shed became a staging post for condemned locomotives awaiting the cutter's torch at the near-at-hand Crewe Works and engines were stored here from many points of the London Midland Region. One such locomotive is former London and North Western Railway Class 7F 0-8-0 No 48964 (21B Bescot) which is dead in the yard on 8th April 1962, the same month as its condemnation. (N.L.Browne)

28) An almost deserted scene at the north end of Crewe (South) shed on 6th September 1962. Present in the frame (left) is 0-6-0 Diesel Shunter No 12025 and an unidentified LMS Class 5 4-6-0. The centrepiece is of BR Class 5 4-6-0 No 73092 a visitor to the shed from 85C Gloucester (Barnwood). This locomotive, once of 10C Patricroft, was one of a numerical batch of the class which were drafted to 84G Shrewsbury in September 1958. (D.K.Jones)

29) Amongst the legions of locomotive types shedded at 5B the most common were LMS Class 5 4-6-0's and LMS Class 8F 2-8-0's. One of the latter, No 48450, from 2C Stourbridge, is in light steam in filthy external condition on 2nd June 1965. For many years No 48450 was a Western Region engine working from such depots as 82B St.Philip's Marsh and 86C Cardiff (Canton). It survived in service until September 1967 being withdrawn from 8A Edge Hill (Liverpool). (D.K.Jones)

30) Amongst the traction on view in the yard at 5B on 28th September 1958 are a duet of LMS Unrebuilt *Patriot* Class 4-6-0's. In steam on the left is No 45502 *Royal Naval Division*, from 12B Carlisle (Upperby) . To the right of No 45502 and out of steam is 8A Edge Hill (Liverpool) based No 45518 *Bradshaw*. The former locomotive succumbed to modernisation in September 1960, followed by *Bradshaw* in October 1962. (N.L.Browne)

31) Until 10th August 1963 most former Western Region types which reached Crewe were despatched to the small shed at Gresty Lane for servicing. The day after the closure of Gresty Lane, Crewe (South) hosts an unfamiliar sight, that of GWR 2800 Class 2-8-0 No 3840, allocated to 81E Didcot which had presumably arrived at Crewe via Shrewsbury. During the last year or so of its working life No 3840 was based at sheds in South Wales. (T.R.Amos)

32) Although an inmate of the more prestigious depot of 5A Crewe (North) LMS *Royal Scot* Class 4-6-0 No 46134 *The Cheshire Regiment* stands in the shed yard at 5B after being serviced on an unknown day in March 1961. In October of this same year *The Cheshire Regiment* was drafted to 8A Edge Hill (Liverpool). It remained there until June of the following year when it went north to 12B Carlisle (Upperby), being withdrawn five months later. (N.E.Preedy)

33) LMS Hughes Class 6P5F 2-6-0 No 42778, a local inhabitant, is photographed in fairly presentable external condition in the yard at Crewe (South) on 8th April 1962 in the company of an unidentified LMS Class 8F 2-8-0 and another 5B engine, LMS Class 3F 0-6-0T No 47400. Between January 1957 and September 1962 a total of twenty-five members of the Hughes Class 6P5F 2-6-0's were based at 5B, though not all at the same time. (N.L.Browne)

34) A brace of elderly former Midland Railway Class 2F 0-6-0's 'grace' the former London and North Western Railway tracks within the shed confines at Crewe (South) on 28th September 1958. Nearest the camera is locally based No 58271 which for a short period of time between May and October 1957 was employed within Crewe Works as a shunter. In May 1959 it moved on to its last abode at 3E Monument Lane in Birmingham. (N.L.Browne)

35) After the closure of the North shed to steam in June 1965 the surviving BR *Britannia* Class 4-6-2's once based at 5A were moved to the South shed and along with the examples allocated to sheds in North Wales and at Carlisle continued to put in stirring performances on passenger trains for another two years or so. One of the fleet of 12A Carlisle (Kingmoor) *Britannia's*, No 70010 *Owen Glendower* is noted in the yard at 5B on 2nd June 1967. (N.E.Preedy)

36) As mentioned in a previous caption Crewe (South) shed was a dumping ground for locomotives awaiting the final call to the workshops for cutting up and amongst the more glamorous types were the famed LMS *Princess* Class 4-6-2's of which all but three were scrapped at their place of birth. On 10th December 1961, two months after withdrawal, No 46211 *Queen Maud* lies unwanted in a section of the yard. It was scrapped in April 1962. (J.M.Tolson)

37) We take our leave of Crewe (South) shed, closed on 6th November 1967, with this shot of LMS Stanier Class 6P5F 2-6-0 No 42977, a local steed, in steam on 8th April 1962. A large number of these engines were based at 5B, the last example disappearing in November 1964. No 42977 took its leave of the shed in August 1962, moving to 21C Bushbury. It later served at 5D Stoke, 8F Springs Branch Wigan, 9G Gorton and 9E Trafford Park. (N.L.Browne)

38) At its height Crewe Locomotive Works was the largest on the London, Midland and Scottish Railway and although still with us today is a shadow of its former self. In the days of steam it was not uncommon for enthusiasts specials to penetrate the Works with their consignments of 'spotters'. On a gloomy 6th August 1964 LMS *Jubilee* Class 4-6-0 No 45672 *Anson* departs with an 'Open Day' special and passes two of the Works shunters. (C.Stacey)

39) There can hardly have been a more 'basic' looking locomotive than the ex. London and North Western Railway Class 1F 0-4-2 Bissel Tank, of which No 47862 was the last surviving example. When recorded for posterity by the photographer, alongside the 'Signal and Tin Shop' at Crewe Works on 4th December 1949, it was still seven years short of retirement. Note the peculiar looking trailing wheel and spartan cab. (A.N.H.Glover)

40) As a logical development of the London and North Western Railway '17 inch goods' came the Class 2F 'Cauliflower' 0-6-0's with larger cylinders and wheels, although there was still little protection for the footplate crews from the elements. Of the 310 examples built from 1880 to 1902, sixty-nine came into BR ownership, some surviving until 1955. No 58413 is photographed at Crewe Works at the time of withdrawal in January 1954. (N.L.Browne)

41) 'Ooops'! - No doubt there were a lot of forms to be filled in and a 'scapegoat' to be found who was responsible for the collision damage to this locomotive. LMS Hughes Class 6P5F 2-6-0 No 42881 has been reduced to a rather bedraggled 0-6-0 wheel arrangement as it awaits repairs at Crewe Works on 7th February 1960. One of a numerical batch (Nos 42881-84) allocated to 12A Carlisle (Kingmoor) it remained in service until November 1962. (A.N.H.Glover)

42) The first Beyer-Garratt 2-6-0 + 0-6-2's were introduced into service on the LMS in 1927, with a further thirty being delivered in 1931. Despite improvements from the original design they were always heavy on coal consumption and maintenance which probably explains why they were all gone by April 1958. On an unknown date in the mid-fifties No 47998, from either 18A Toton or 18C Hasland, basks in weak sunshine at Crewe Works. (R.Butterfield)

43) All types of LMS and BR Standard Classes visited Crewe Works for light repairs, heavy overhauls and scrapping over the years. With a section of the paint shop in the background LMS Class 8F 2-8-0 No 48630, from 5B Crewe (South), looks immaculate after overhaul on 17th June 1962. Before being returned to its home base No 48630 was employed briefly as a Works shunter 'WI4'. It was condemned from Crewe (South) in July 1965. (N.E.Preedy)

44) The Works shunters at Crewe mostly consisted of former Midland Railway and LMS 0-6-0's and 0-6-0 Tanks along with examples of 0-6-0's and 0-6-0 Saddle Tanks from the former Lancashire and Yorkshire Railway like this one seen here on 24th May 1955, No 51446 which was withdrawn in February 1962. Also employed as shunters until October 1960 were two former Caledonian Railway Class 0F 0-4-0 Saddle Tanks, Nos 56027 and 56032. (R.Butterfield)

45) An immaculate looking *LMS Royal Scot* Class 4-6-0 No 46117 *Welsh Guardsman*, from 20A Leeds (Holbeck), waits to be steamed and returned to its home depot from Crewe Works on 15th March 1953. Holbeck shed belonged to the London Midland Region of British Railways from 1948-1957 after which it was taken over by the North Eastern Region and coded 55A. After brief spells at 56F Low Moor and 56D Mirfield, No 46117 was to die at Holbeck in late 1962. (B.K.B.Green)

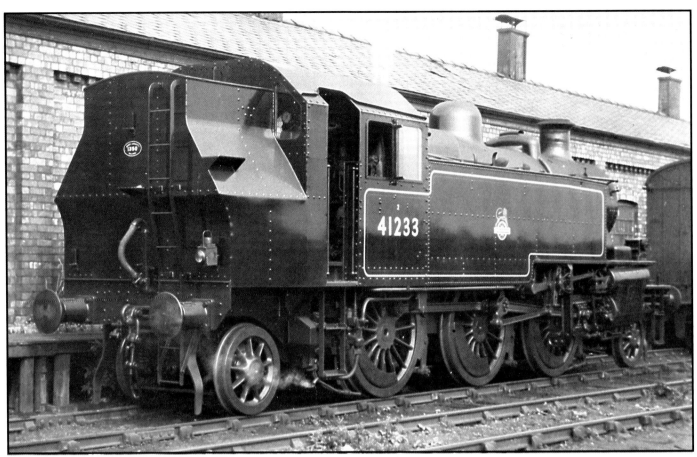

46) Possibly brand new, LMS Ivatt Class 2 2-6-2T No 41233 is employed as a Works shunter at Crewe on 29th August 1949. Apart from the other locomotives already mentioned as being regular shunters at Crewe Works there were also a batch of BR Class 2 2-6-2 Tanks Nos 84021-24 (July 1962 to September 1964). The steam aspects of shunting, so common for countless years came to an end in October 1966. (B.K.B.Green)

47) The magnificent LMS *Royal Scot* Class 4-6-0's were originally built with Fowler boilers as seen in this photograph of No 46164 *The Artist's Rifleman* noted in the Works yard at Crewe on 26th February 1950. All of the members of the class were later rebuilt with taper boilers under the direction of C.E.Fairburn. They were noted for their rough riding, but their high qualities of free steaming and abilities to haul heavy loads was never in doubt. (A.N.H.Glover)

48) With the object in the foreground looking like an oversized German soldier's helmet ex. London and North Western Railway Class 7F 0-8-0 No 49048 waits to be reunited with its tender at Crewe Works on a sun-filled 28th November 1954. In the background is an unidentified LMS *Royal Scot* Class 4-6-0. No 49048, based in its later life at 5C Stafford and 5B Crewe (South), became an early victim of modernisation being condemned in November 1959. (A.N.H.Glover)

49) We end our sojourn to Crewe with this photograph of the last steam locomotive built for British Railways, BR Class 9F 2-10-0 No 92220 *Evening Star* inside the new paint shop on 20th August 1967 after restoration. Crewe Works ceased normal repairs on steam locomotives when the now preserved BR *Britannia* Class 4-6-2 No 70013 *Oliver Cromwell*, from 12A Carlisle (Kingmoor), was released into traffic in a flag waving ceremony on 2nd February 1967. (F.Hornby)

50) Lumps of coal and other obstructions litter the foreground at Doncaster shed, coded 36A, as an elderly and smoke-stained former Great Eastern Railway J69 Class 0-6-0T No 68507, a local engine, shunts a mixed bag of stock on 10th May 1960. No 68507, from a design of Holden's back in 1902, is almost life-expired and is eking out its last days of existence. Condemned the following month it was soon destined to be cut up at Doncaster Works. (D.K.Jones)

51) We now turn our attention to the days of steam at Doncaster station under the ownership of British Railways. Light steam drifts from the whistle of LNER A4 Class 4-6-2 No 60009 *Union of South Africa*, from 64B Haymarket, as it approaches the camera with the 10.08 am express from Kings Cross to Edinburgh (Waverley) on 22nd August 1954. Equipped with a double chimney in November 1958, No 60009 went straight into preservation in June 1966. (R.Butterfield)

52) What a 'feast' for the young spotters gathered together on a platform at Doncaster station on 20th July 1957. Coupled together after overhaul at the nearby Workshops are, from left to right:- LNER K3 Class 2-6-0 No 61824 (38A Colwick), LMS Ivatt Class 4 2-6-0 No 43099 (53A Hull - Dairycoates), LNER Al Class 4-6-2 No 60143 *Sir Walter Scott* (52A Gateshead), LNER K3 Class 2-6-0 No 61906 (52B Heaton) and LNER 02 Class 2-8-0 No 63969 (36A Doncaster). (B.W.L.Brooksbank)

53) A splendid panoramic view of Doncaster station with a host of tracks and cross-overs, although the only manual signal in sight is the 'dummy' in the foreground. Arriving with an unidentified express, including a GUV (General Utility Vehicle) is a locally based LNER B1 Class 4-6-0 No 61196 seen passing some mixed stock. Based at 36A for many a year, No 61196 was withdrawn in September 1965 and cut up later at Wards, Beighton. (Peter Hay)

54) Steam leaks from many outlets as LNER V2 Class 2-6-2 No 60814, from 34A Kings Cross, sets off on a sun-filled day on 19th July 1954 from Doncaster with the 9.22 am York to Kings Cross express. The lengthy footbridge in the background connects the station to the Works. No 60814 made its leave of 34A in June 1962 moving north to 34F Grantham. Condemned in April 1963 it was scrapped two months later at its birthplace of Doncaster. (N.E.Preedy)

55) Exactly the same location but with a different locomotive. On the opposite platform are a gaggle of spotters suitably equipped with notebooks and 'duffle bags' as they endure a hard day's spotting. Already noted in their books is this 'stranger-in-the-camp' from the North Eastern Region. The footplate crew of LNER B16/2 No 61455, from 50A York, look towards the camera as their filthy charge heads a parcels train on 4th June 1963. (H.L.Holland)

56) In direct contrast to the previous two photographs the next scene is set in dismal and rainy conditions with hardly a soul to be seen. 56C Copley Hill based LNER A1 Class 4-6-2 No 60117 *Bois Roussel* waits patiently in Doncaster station with a northbound passenger train. After the demise of Copley Hill shed in September 1964 this British Railways built Pacific (1948) was transferred to 56B Ardsley where it was withdrawn in June 1965. (D.K.Jones)

57) In a neglected travel-stained condition, 34A Kings Cross allocated LNER A4 Class 4-6-2 No 60003 *Andrew K. McCosh* steams past Doncaster South signalbox as it arrives at Doncaster on 8th July 1962 with the 10.00 am express from Kings Cross to Leeds. Constructed in 1937 as No 4494 this engine originally carried the name of *Osprey*. It was modified with a double chimney in July 1957 and was one of the first to be withdrawn in December 1962. (J.M.Tolson)

58) Another British Railways constructed Pacific was A1 Class 4-6-2 No 60114 *W.P.Allen* which saw out its short working life (sixteen years) from the Motive Power Depots at Copley Hill, Grantham and Doncaster. On a sunny but unknown date in 1957 it is in charge of an up express bound for Peterborough and London. Withdrawn from 36A in December 1964 it lay in store for several months before being despatched to Hughes Bolckows of North Blyth. (N.E.Preedy)

59) Despite it being at the height of the summer service this platform at Doncaster is totally deserted and only a handful of carriages occupy the sidings in the right of the frame. The only object to disturb the stillness is LNER V2 Class 2-6-2 No 60870, from the nearby shed at 36A, as it basks light engine in the warm sunshine on 5th August 1962. Condemned in July 1963, No 60870 was cut up almost straight away at Doncaster Works. (J.Schatz)

60) A short distance from Doncaster (home of the St.Leger) is Black Carr Junction with lines leading to and from Gainsborough etc. With the signalman observing from within his domain a Doncaster bound express swings round the curve and onto the main line. In charge of this express is LNER B17 'Sandringham' Class 4-6-0 No 61626 *Brancepath Castle*, from 31B March, on 28th June 1952. By January 1960 this locomotive had disappeared into history. (R.W.Hinton)

61) 36A Doncaster was a massive shed by any standards and housed a host of steam locomotives from a wide variety of classes. Lined up in front of one end of the depot are an unidentified LNER A4 Class 4-6-2, LNER A1 Class 4-6-2 No 60148 *Aboyeur* (56C Copley Hill), English Electric Type 4 Diesel No D387 and a begrimed LNER B1 Class 4-6-0 on 28th April 1963. *Aboyeur* ended its working life from 56B Ardsley, being rendered redundant in June 1965. (F.Hornby)

62) Two footplatemen and a fitter go about their daily business in the railway dress so common to steam days, but which can still be seen today on preserved railways. All three are near to 34A Kings Cross based LNER A4 Class 4-6-2 No 60029 *Woodcock* at the London end of Doncaster shed on 23rd July 1961. *Woodcock*, modified with a double chimney in October 1958 moved from Kings Cross shed to 34E New England in June 1963 and was withdrawn four months later. (N.E.Preedy)

63) The overwhelming allocation of steam locomotives at 36A were from LNER origins, along with many representatives of the War Department 2-8-0's and BR Class 9F 2-10-0's. There were however, the oddity or two, such as the engine pictured here, former Midland Railway Class 1F 0-6-0T No 41779 noted on 17th June 1956. For No 41779 the writing was on the wall with condemnation looming in July 1957, being taken to Derby Works for scrapping. (A.N.H.Glover)

64) With the offices of the shed clerical staff/booking clerks etc., providing a backdrop, former Great Central Railway 04/8 Class 2-8-0 No 63720 takes a well earned rest between duties at 36A on 9th June 1963. Facing No 63720 is LNER B1 Class 4-6-0 No 61059 a visitor to the depot from 31B March. This engine was taken into Departmental Stock after withdrawal in November 1963 a process which extended its working life until April 1966. (D.K.Jones)

65) Although the tender is stacked to the brim with coal supplies it is the end of the road for Gresley inspired A3 Class 4-6-2 No 60107 *Royal Lancer* after withdrawal from 34F Grantham seen with other stored locomotives at Doncaster shed on 8th September 1963. Constructed in 1923 *Royal Lancer* had a life of some forty years and received a double chimney in June 1959 and German smoke deflectors in February 1962. It was cut up in October 1963. (K.L.Seal)

66) By 8th May 1965 the steam stock at 36A had been considerably reduced, but there was still much of interest to be seen. LMS Hughes Class 6P5F 2-6-0 No 42715, from far off 9G Gorton in Manchester, is an unusual choice for a Warwickshire Railway Society visit to Doncaster. Records show that from January 1957 onwards No 42715 was allocated to the sheds at Newton Heath (twice), Bolton, Wigan L & Y (twice), Aintree (twice), Gorton and Stockport. (D.Webster)

67) In common with many of the larger depots on the Eastern Region much of the rostered work was freight orientated and the Riddles WD Class 8F 2-8-0's were frequent visitors to 36A from other sheds within the region. On 21st July 1963 No 90719, from 41D Canklow, looks in fine fettle in the shed yard at 36A, where it is sporting 'express' headcodes! In the background is an unidentified LNER V2 Class 2-6-2. (T.R.Amos)

68) The powerful LNER 02 Class 2-8-0's were designed purely for freight duties and were often found as far north as York and despite the mass introduction of diesel power they were not affected by withdrawals until 1960. From then onwards the class was decimated and rendered extinct by October 1963. On 29th June 1958 No 63969, a local inhabitant of 36A, is seen out of steam. Its revenue earning days came to an end from 36E Retford. (A.N.H.Glover)

69) With the crude and disused wooden coaling stage in the background we espy an example of modern steam traction in the shape of 1953 built BR *Britannia* Class 4-6-2 No 70035 *Rudyard Kipling*, of 31B March, in the shed yard at Doncaster on 8th September 1963. The once common sight of these Pacifics on Doncaster shed were soon to become a thing of the past with the transfer of the Eastern Region based examples to the LMR in December 1963. (K.L.Seal)

70) Apart from the LNER A1 Class 4-6-2's based on the Eastern Region examples from North Eastern Region sheds like 50A York were frequent visitors to Doncaster. With a WD Class 2-8-0 in the background No 60150 *Willbrook* poses in the sunshine at Doncaster on 1st May 1961. Built in 1949 by British Railways *Willbrook* spent the last few years of its working life at 52A Gateshead as well as York prior to the end in October 1964. (N.E.Preedy)

71) As mentioned in an earlier caption Doncaster had more than its fair share of BR Class 9F 2-10-0's and often hosted 'foreigners' from other depots. One such 'foreigner' seen in the depot yard on 18th May 1959 is No 92178, from 34E New England and equipped with a double chimney. Introduced into service at 34E in September 1958, No 92178 was drafted to a final home at 41J Langwith Junction in January 1965. (N.E.Preedy)

72) Once of 32A Norwich, LNER K3 Class 2-6-0 No 61812 found itself on the books at 36A by February 1957 where it remained until withdrawal in September 1962, being cut up almost immediately at the nearby Works. Behind No 61812 on a sunny day in 1960 is another Doncaster locomotive, LNER V2 Class 2-6-2 No 60936 which was also condemned in September 1962. In the background we can see the clean lines of an LNER A3 Class 4-6-2. (N.E.Preedy)

73) The first port of call for most if not all of the locomotives outshopped at Doncaster was to the shed at 36A prior to despatching to their home bases. This British Railways built (1949) Pacific LNER A2 Class 4-6-2 No 60537 *Bachelor's Button*, from 64B Haymarket, has had its last overhaul prior to withdrawal as it stands outside the running shed on 15th October 1961. Condemnation from Haymarket for No 60537 came in December 1962. (J.M.Tolson)

74) Large lumps of coal litter the foreground at Doncaster shed on an undesignated date in 1960. Another locomotive fresh from overhaul at the Works is K1 Class 2-6-0 No 62066, of 31B March. This was another class which appeared after British Railways was formed and their ranks remained intact until 1963. Some members survived until the end of steam on the North Eastern Region in 1967. No 62066 was withdrawn in January 1965. (N.E.Preedy)

75) The shed roof looks in a state of disrepair on 25th September 1955 where steam issues from one of the cylinder cocks of LNER V2 Class 2-6-2 No 60872 *King's* Own *Yorkshire Light Infantry*, a local steed. Except for a brief period, July to September 1961, when No 60872 was based at 34F Grantham, it remained at 36A, being withdrawn in September 1963. In the right of the frame is WD Class 8F 2-8-0 No 90538 another inmate at Doncaster. (N.E.Preedy)

76) LNER B1 Class 4-6-0 No 61158 did not have far to travel after overhaul being based at 36A where it is seen in the yard on 25th October 1959. It was destined to remain here until no longer being required by the operating authorities after the closure of the shed to steam in April 1966. All of its surviving steam stock was withdrawn and sent for cutting up although the depot retained its servicing facilities for visiting engines. (N.E.Preedy)

77) We turn our attentions to Doncaster Works, known as 'The Plant', which was first established as early as 1853 and by the late fifties covered some 93 acres. Like Crewe Works it too employed its own shunters like LNER J50 Class 0-6-0T No 68917 which had been transferred into Departmental Stock in September 1962 and renumbered No 12. Built at Doncaster in 1919 it is seen in steam at the Works on 28th April 1963 complete with its crew. (F.Hornby)

78) A wheelbarrow and an assortment of other items clutter the foreground at Doncaster Works on 23rd July 1961. Looking in superb external condition after overhaul is 41A Sheffield (Darnall) based LNER B1 Class 4-6-0 No 61056 which will soon be steamed and despatched home. This locomotive remained at Darnall until November 1962, transferring its allegiance to 40B Immingham from whence it was taken out of traffic in April 1964. (N.E.Preedy)

79) A variety of bits and pieces associated with steam locomotives are scattered on the ground in front of two LNER A3 Class 4-6-2's Nos 60112 *St.Simon* (34F Grantham) and 60062 *Minoru* (34E New England) as they pose outside a major building at Doncaster Works on 27th January 1962 prior to being overhauled. Nos 60062 and 60112, once regular inmates at 34A Kings Cross, were withdrawn together at the end of 1964 from 34E New England shed. (P.A.Rowlings)

80) Doncaster Works was responsible for constructing many famous and not so famous locomotive types for the LNER and beyond into British Railways days. Coming into the latter category were the BR Class 4 2-6-0's like No 76109 seen in a brand new condition on 18th August 1957. It was released into traffic the following month and allocated to 62A Thornton Junction. It remained in Scotland for all of its short life, being condemned in September 1966. (W.G.Boyden)

81) As well as being responsible for the building and overhaul of steam engines (and wagons) Doncaster also cut them up by the hundreds from many parts of the British Railways system. In the 'rush to modernise' the LNER B2/B17 'Sandringham' Class 4-6-0's became early casualties and many examples ended their days at Doncaster. B17/4 No 61648 *Arsenal*, once of 30A Stratford and withdrawn in December 1958 awaits its fate on 12th April 1959. (A.N.H.Glover)

82) A brace of LNER A3 Class 4-6-2's Nos 60037 *Hyperion*, from far-off 64A St. Margarets (Edinburgh), and 60066 *Merry Hampton* (34A Kings Cross) have been overhauled (possibly for the last time) as they await their return to service in the Works yard on 19th May 1962. Both are in final BR condition with double chimneys and German pattern smoke deflectors. Both locomotives were destined to die towards the end of 1963. (R.W.Hinton)

83) It was a fact of life, especially under British Railways, that freight engines were usually seen in a grimy and work-stained condition. About the only time they were in immaculate condition was when they were fresh from overhaul. Former Great Central Railway O1 Class 2-8-0 No 63746 (31B March), introduced by Thompson in 1944, is in classic 'eat your dinner off it condition' minus coal supplies at 'The Plant' on l9th May 1962. (R.Leitch)

84) Bright sunshine highlights the simple lines of Thompson LNER A2/1 Class 4-6-2 No 60509 *Waverley*, from 64B Haymarket, as it stands lifeless in the Works yard on 9th May 1954. With the advent of mainline diesels the earlier members of the A2's were decimated with Nos 60501 to 60510 being withdrawn between November 1959 and July 1961. All were cut up without exception at Doncaster Works, in August 1960 in the case of *Waverley*. (R.Butterfield)

85) Transferred from 34B Hornsey to 36A Doncaster in July 1961 LNER J50 Class 0-6-0T No 68928 is in disgraceful external condition in the Works yard on 27th January 1962. By September of this year No 68928 was taken into Departmental Stock and renumbered No 13, surviving in this guise until May 1965 as a Works shunter well after steam repairs had ceased at Doncaster. Lurking in the background is BR *Britannia* Class 4-6-2 No 70006 *Robert Burns*. (P.A.Rowlings)

86) Although allocated to 30A Stratford in London, which had its own workshops, LNER B1 Class 4-6-0 No 61378 has made the expensive journey to Doncaster for overhaul and poses for the camera on a wet 2nd July 1961. Constructed by the North British Locomotive Company in 1951, No 61378 spent most if not all of its active life at sheds on the Eastern Region which also included the ones at 30F Parkeston and 31B March as well as Stratford. (N.E.Preedy)

87) We end this photo coverage of Doncaster Works with the sad sight of two locomotives which will never be steamed again. In the first frame, taken on 19th May 1962, is the freshly condemned Gresley inspired LNER K3/2 Class 2-6-0 No 61922, built in 1924 and latterly of 50B Hull (Dairycoates). No 61922 still carries number and shedplates. It was quite often the case that intrepid spotters used to remove these items as souvenirs. (R.Leitch)

88) This second sequence is of LNER A2/3 Class 4-6-2 No 60514 *Chamossaire* (34E New England) seen in a neglected condition on 14th October 1962, two months before 'official' withdrawal. The repair of steam locomotives ceased at 'The Plant' during early November 1963 when WD Class 8F 2-8-0 No 90153 (41D Canklow) and LNER A4 Class 4-6-2 No 60009 *Union of South Africa* of 61B Aberdeen (Ferryhill) were turned out, with the latter being the last to leave. (J.M.Tolson)

89) The SR D15 Class were Drummond's last and best 4-4-0's. In April 1952 No 30464 is working a Portsmouth to Salisbury stopping service, here entering Eastleigh's up loop platform. The riveted mass in the left of the picture is the upright of structure No 201c, the great signal gantry which spanned the main lines at the south end of Eastleigh station. No 30464 was withdrawn in 1954 after an active summer hauling Saturday Waterloo to Lymington Pier through trains. (Peter Hay)

90) In this photograph we have a broader view of the same signal gantry at Eastleigh on 1st August 1962 during the school holidays which explains why so many spotters are present as well as one or two older members of the public. SR *King Arthur* Class 4-6-0 No 30770 *Sir Prianius*, a local steed from 71A, is the subject of much admiration as it stands light engine in the station. In the left of the frame is a Bulleid Pacific. (N.L.Browne)

91) The date is 6th September 1964 and we espy another light engine, this time in the shape of SR Rebuilt *West Country* Class 4-6-2 No 34008 *Padstow*, another Eastleigh locomotive which was constructed in September 1945 and rebuilt at Eastleigh Works in July 1960. Records show us that from January 1957 onwards *Padstow* was based at the sheds at 70A Nine Elms (twice) and 75A Brighton as well as at Eastleigh. It was condemned in June 1967. (B.K.B.Green)

92) Former Great Western Railway locomotives were not infrequent visitors to Eastleigh from the Western Region. On 24th April 1958 GWR 2251 Class 0-6-0 No 3210, from 81E Didcot, stands beneath the smartly maintained enclosed footbridge with a homebound local passenger from Southampton via Newbury. No 3210 spent the last few years of its life on the former Somerset and Dorset Railway based at Templecombe shed until November 1964. (F.Hornby)

93) The SR S15 Class 4-6-0's were designed for mixed traffic duties and were maids of all work. The 30496-30515 series were developed from the N15 Class *(King Arthur)* and were without exception based at 70B Feltham in London. In April 1952 No 30496 trails a lengthy freight train through Eastleigh station on a centre road. Of this batch of S15's Nos 30499 and 30506 are preserved, whereas No 30496 was cut up at Eastleigh Works in August 1963. (Peter Hay)

94) Taken from the lofty vantage point of the road bridge (entrance to Eastleigh shed and works) to the west of the station, we can just make out part of the shed in the distance as SR Unrebuilt *West Country* Class 4-6-2 No 34006 *Bude*, from 70A Nine Elms, leaves a trail of black exhaust as it steams towards the camera with an up express in the summer of 1954. *Bude* survived to within a matter of months before the end of Southern steam. (D.K.Jones)

95) The H15 Class 4P5F 4-6-0's, first introduced in 1914, were a mixture of designs by both Maunsell and Urie and were employed on a wide variety of trains. On 21st April 1956 No 30484, of 70A Nine Elms, is employed at Eastleigh station on a westbound local stopping service. These engines were soon to become life-expired and all were gone from the railway scene by December 1961. No 30484 disappeared for ever in May 1959. (N.E.Preedy)

96) A variety of domestic properties look upon the railway scene at Eastleigh as SR M7 Class 0-4-4T No 30032, a local engine, glides into a platform with a three-coach local passenger train on 14th May 1953. Reallocated to 70A Nine Elms in December 1958, No 30032 spent a number of years there before returning to Eastleigh shed for a last spell in March 1963. After withdrawal four months later it was despatched to a scrapyard in Kent. (D.K.Jones)

97) One of the legion of SR S15 Class 4-6-0's allocated to 70B Feltham, No 30839, passes a signalbox and heads light engine through Eastleigh station for servicing at the local depot on a bright and sunny day on 13th October 1963. Of the twenty-five five members of this batch of S15's (Nos 30823-47) some five examples were salvaged by the preservation movement. Unfortunately No 30839 was not one of them, being cut up during 1966. (N.E.Preedy)

98) Constructed during April 1945 and rebuilt in March 1957, SR *Merchant Navy* Class 4-6-2 No 35017 *Belgian Marine*, from 70A Nine Elms, passes a diesel multiple unit and speeds in a westbound direction with a down express seen on a through road at Eastleigh on 6th September 1960. Transferred to a last home at 70G Weymouth in September 1964, *Belgian Marine* was withdrawn in July 1966 and scrapped at Buttigiegs, Newport two months later. (B.K.B.Green)

99) During the summer months of the early and mid-sixties former GWR locomotives were often employed on through trains from Oxford to Bournemouth and Weymouth. Looking in a shoddy condition, minus most identifying plates, GWR *Modified* Class 4-6-0 No 7927 *Willington Hall*, of 86B Newport (Ebbw Junction), is well off its home territory at Eastleigh with a Newcastle to Bournemouth express on 11th August 1965. (D.K.Jones)

100) With some steam activity going on in the far distance there appears to be more characters of the 'spotting fraternity' on the platform at Eastleigh than passengers on a sun-filled 1st August 1962. The centre of attention is a smartly maintained 21A Saltley (Birmingham) based BR Class 9F 2-10-0 No 92129 as it runs through light engine. In August 1964, No 92129 bade farewell to Saltley shed, moving south to a new abode at 2D Banbury. (N.L.Browne)

101) A murky day at Eastleigh station - circa 1960. A plume of white smoke erupts from the funnel of SR *Schools* Class 4-4-0 No 30910 *Merchant Taylors* (70A Nine Elms) as it tows a 2500hp Class 71 third rail electric locomotive No E5001 through Eastleigh station. Note the 'Southern Railway' warning notice still in situ in the left of the picture. *Merchant Taylors* is no longer with us, but No E5001 is preserved today. (R.S.Carpenter)

102) There is a change of footplate crew at platform 4 at Eastleigh on an unknown date in the late fifties where the railwaymen mingle amidst an assortment of spotters. 81E Didcot based GWR 2251 Class 0-6-0 No 2252 is being employed on a Didcot - Newbury - Southampton service. This locomotive was destined to be amongst the first examples of the class to be condemned, from Didcot shed in December 1959. It was cut up during 1960. (R.S.Carpenter)

103) Despite the gloomy conditions and the presence of a spotter it is a summer's day when this picture was taken. Under clear signals an unidentified BR Class 5 4-6-0 heads a westbound freight through Eastleigh station on 1st July 1965 where in the distance we can make out a single 0-6-0 Diesel Shunter. Eastleigh station, some seventy-three miles from Waterloo, ceased its association with steam locomotion in early July 1967. (D.K.Jones)

104) Eastleigh shed of London and South Western Railway origins was coded 71A and 70D under British Railways and was a large open-ended running structure. Fresh from a heavy overhaul at the nearby workshops on 15th May 1954 is 74B Ramsgate based SR *Schools* Class 4-4-0 No 30913 *Christ's Hospital* awaiting steaming and despatch to its home shed. To the left of *Christ's Hospital* is SR 02 Class 0-4-4T No 30233 an Eastleigh locomotive. (B.K.B.Green)

105) A trio of locomotives are outside part of the running shed at Eastleigh on a dull 10th November 1963. In the left of the frame is a SR 2-6-0. In the centre is SR Rebuilt *Merchant Navy* Class 4-6-2 No 35001 *Channel Packet*, from 70A Nine Elms, behind which is an unidentified SR *Battle of Britain* Class 4-6-2. After condemnation from 70F Bournemouth in November 1964, No 35001 was despatched to Birds, Morriston, Swansea for scrapping. (N.L.Browne)

106) With its smokebox door wide open to the elements and sporting a 'NOT TO BE MOVED' notice on the bufferbeam, BR Class 4 2-6-0 No 76017, a local engine, is photographed in the yard at 71A on 18th May 1955. In March 1960 No 76017 was transferred to 72B Salisbury a depot it was to remain at until rendered redundant in July 1965. After many years rotting away at Barry Docks it was saved for posterity by the Mid-Hants Railway. (N.L.Browne)

107) A severe shortage of coal supplies in the winter of 1946 led to oil firing conversions in 1947 but once our foreign exchange reserves ran out we could not afford to purchase any more oil. Few, if any of the converted engines ever did any useful work. Among them was SR L11Class 4-4-0 No 411, seen here amongst the weeds on a scrap road at Eastleigh in April 1952 after being stored for several years. It was cut up later in the year. (Peter Hay)

108) An unidentified SR *Lord Nelson* Class 4-6-0 lurks in the background of this picture, taken on 30th August 1951. In the foreground looking in fine fettle but carrying no logo of ownership is SR M7 Class 0-4-4T No 30378 which is out of steam in the shed yard at Eastleigh. In June 1959 No 30378 was moved to 70C Guildford and in March 1962 to a final home at 71B Bournemouth. It was taken out of service at the end of 1962. (B.K.B.Green)

109) Constructed at the height of the Second World War at Ashford Works, SR Bulleid Q1 Class 0-6-0 No 33021, an Eastleigh loco, shows off its very basic design in the shed yard on 6th October 1960. These wartime engines were very powerful and employed on heavy freight workings. They were untouched by withdrawals until 1963, but all were gone by the beginning of 1966. One example No 33001, withdrawn in May 1964, is now preserved. (F.Hornby)

110) A trio of ex.works locomotives are lined up in the shed yard at Eastleigh on 6th September 1955. Leading the line-up is SR Unrebuilt *Merchant Navy* Class 4-6-2 No 35025 *Brocklebank Line*, from 72A Exmouth Junction, behind which is a SR Unrebuilt *West Country* Class 4-6-2 and a SR *Lord Nelson* Class 4-6-0. During the late fifties, *Brocklebank Line*, rebuilt in December 1956, was drafted to 71B Bournemouth. It ended its days at Exmouth Junction. (B.K.B.Green)

111) Another Bulleid Pacific in exemplary external condition is noted near to a GWR type in the yard at 71A. Facing the camera is SR Unrebuilt *West Country* Class 4-6-2 No 34045 *Ottery St.Mary*, of 75A Brighton, seen on 6th September 1956. Like *Brocklebank Line* in the previous picture *Ottery St.Mary* was also rebuilt, in October 1958. It made its departure from Brighton shed in August 1958, moving to 70A Nine Elms and then to 71B Bournemouth three months later (B.K.B.Green)

112) Eastleigh shed had a small number of Maunsell designed (1938) SR 0 Class 0-6-0's on its books during the fifties including No 30543, seen here in steam in the yard on 15th May 1954. They were employed in the main on freight duties and the class remained intact until the end of 1962. During the last two years of its life No 30543 had four different abodes, at 75D Stewarts Lane, 75E Three Bridges, 75A Brighton and 75B Redhill. (B.K.B.Green

113) What magnificent beasts the SR *Merchant Navy* Class 4-6-2's were before they were rebuilt by British Railways. Unfortunately for the author he never saw them in their original guise (too young!). Bright sunshine envelopes the fine proportions of 70A Nine Elms based No 35014 *Nederland Line* in the yard at Eastleigh on 30th August 1951. Rebuilt in July 1956 *Nederland Line* was withdrawn from 70G Weymouth in March 1967. (B.K.B.Green)

114) As the steam stock on the Southern Region was decimated by withdrawals space became available at Eastleigh Works for the overhaul of locomotives from other regions though what precisely LMS *Jubilee* Class 4-6-0 No 45699 *Galatea* was doing here on 7th February 1965 is a bit of a mystery having been withdrawn in November 1964 for it was not cut up here. In for repairs behind No 45699 is LMS Class 8F 2-8-0 No 48471 (6D Shrewsbury). (B.Rands)

15) The Billinton inspired SR K Class 4P5F 2-6-0's were rather unique as they were the only examples that were not designed by Maunsell to survive into the sixties. They were easily distinguishable from other 2-6-0's by virtue of their design. On 30th August 1951 No 32352 (75E Three Bridges) is ex.works at Eastleigh. Although almost 50 years old the class was intact until 1962 during which they were withdrawn en masse. (B.K.B.Green)

116) A feather of steam escapes from GWR 2251 Class 0-6-0 No 2264 (81D Reading) as the fireman sorts out his coal supplies in what appears to be a former Great Central Railway style tender on 18th May 1955 whilst on a visit to Eastleigh shed. These particular locomotives were extremely popular and there was hardly a secondary or branch line on the Western Region which was not graced by their presence. (N.L.Browne)

117) The paintwork gleams and glistens on SR Unrebuilt *West Country* Class 4-6-2 No 34027 *Taw Valley*, from 72A Exmouth Junction, after being released from Eastleigh Works on 30th June 1952. From September 1957 until withdrawal in August 1964 *Taw Valley* was allocated to 73B Bricklayers Arms (twice), 74B Ramsgate, 75A Brighton and 70E Salisbury. Rebuilt in September 1957 it was rescued from Barry Docks by the preservation movement early in 1980. (B.K.B.Green)

118) A duet of tank engines are cast aside on a weed-strewn track at Eastleigh shed on 6th September 1956. Nearest the camera, rusting away, is condemned SR 757 Class 0-6-2T No 30758 *Lord St.Levan*. To the left of No 30758 is SR 02 Class 0-4-4T No 30177 (70B Feltham) which although minus coupling rods lived to steam another day, surviving in service until September 1959. In the far right of the frame is SR *King Arthur* Class 4-6-0 No 30784 *Sir Nerovens*. (B.K.B.Green)

119) This final picture taken at Eastleigh shed is a mixture of old and new with an elderly SR T9 Class 'Greyhound' 4-4-0 No 30288, from 71A, built in February 1900 at Nine Elms, and a BR 200hp 0-6-0 Diesel Shunter No 11223 (built in April 1957) on 26th April 1958. No 30288 was taken out of service during December 1960 and cut up five months later. On 9th July 1967 this famous shed closed its doors to steam for ever. (F.Hornby)

120) The locomotive works at Eastleigh was not established until 1909 some nineteen years after the Carriage and Wagon Works had been transferred here from Nine Elms and all in all a total of 2,600 men were employed. As can be seen in this photograph the erecting shop was a light and airy place. On 31st August 1963 two LMS Class 2 2-6-2 Tanks and a BR Class 5 4-6-0 are in various stages of repair along with the frames of BR Class 4 2-6-0 No 76007. (F.Hornby)

121) Items related to the overhaul of steam locomotives litter the foreground on 23rd May 1965 as two Bulleid Pacifics undergo overhauls in the erecting shop at Eastleigh. Nearest the camera is SR Rebuilt *West Country* Class 4-6-2 No 34098 *Templecombe* (a local engine) behind which is an unidentified SR *Battle of Britain* Class 4-6-2. Rebuilt at Eastleigh in February 1961 *Templecombe* was destined to remain in revenue earning service until June 1967. (D.Webster)

122) Looking extremely grimy and forlorn SR N Class 2-6-0 No 31835, from 72A Exmouth Junction, is minus all of its wheels and has been chocked in readiness for what is possibly its last overhaul on 31st August 1963. Equipped with a BR Class 4 2-6-0 chimney, No 31835 was to be condemned from Exmouth Junction in September 1964. To the left of No 31835 is BR Class 4 2-6-0 No 76025, of 71B Bournemouth, which survived there until October 1965. (F.Hornby)

123) Although cold and silent this is an impressive view of SR *King Arthur* Class 4-6-0 No 30748 *Vivien*, constructed at Eastleigh in August 1922, as it makes a visit to its birthplace on 11th September 1955, some two years away from condemnation from 70D Basingstoke. Although scrapped at Eastleigh in October 1957 the name of *Vivien* was to live on after it was later transferred to BR Class 5 4-6-0 No 73117 in April 1961. (F.Hornby)

124) 'Steam', 'Electric' and an 'Aeroplane' at Eastleigh Works on the afternoon of Tuesday 29th September 1964. As the plane from the nearby airfield zooms over the works, SR USA Class 0-6-0T No DS233, from Redbridge Sleeper Depot, shunts Electric Bo-Bo No E5001 . Based at 71I Southampton Docks for many a year, No DS233 (30061) was transferred into Departmental Stock in November 1962 and survived until the end of steam on the Southern. (J.D.Gomersall)

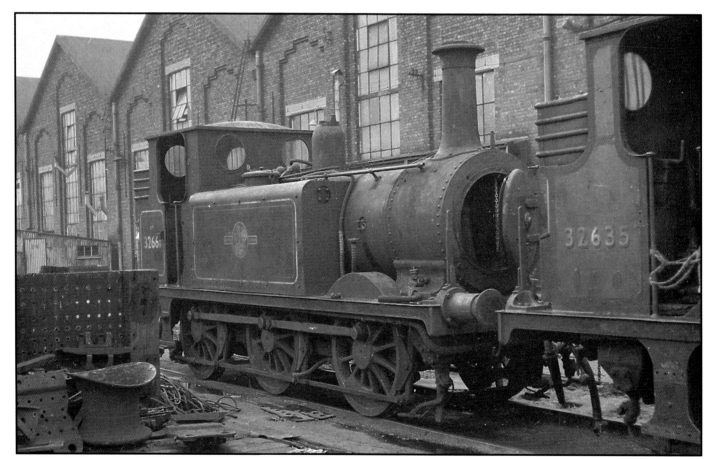

125) Looking forlorn and unwanted two of the diminutive Stroudley SR A1X Class 0-6-0 Tanks rot away alongside the Works building at Eastleigh on 10th April 1963 after withdrawal. Nearest the camera is the former Works shunter at Brighton No 32635 which was transferred from Departmental to normal operating stock (DS377) in January 1959. To the rear of No 32635 is No 32661, once of 71A. Both engines were cut up at Eastleigh in late 1963. (N.L.Browne)

126) In common with all of the major Workshops Eastleigh had separate facilities for the scrapping of locomotives. On a grey day in April 1961 there is the sad sight of dismembered wheels, discarded bogies and tenders and other items of scrap. Awaiting the attentions of the cutter's torch is a bedraggled SR T9 Class 'Greyhound' 4-4-0 No 30729, once of 70F Fratton, 72B Salisbury and latterly of 72A Exmouth Junction in Devon. (T.Wright)

127) Presumably condemned after an accident at Woking, SR N15X Class 4-6-0 No 32327 *Trevithick* displays the damage incurred in a siding at Eastleigh Works on 22nd April 1956. This was one of seven engines rebuilt from the Brighton L Class 4-6-4 Tanks. The 'honour' of being the last locomotive to be outshopped from Eastleigh Works fell to SR Rebuilt *Battle of Britain* Class 4-6-2 No 34089 *602 Squadron* which left on 3rd October 1966. (R.W.Hinton)

128) We now move on to the last location in this album, that of Swindon, some seventy-seven miles from Paddington and the junction for the line to Gloucester. Smoke and steam is highlighted by the crisp winter air on 7th February 1960 as begrimed GWR *Hall* Class 4-6-0 No 6900 *Abney Hall*, from 82B St.Philip's Marsh, passes a section of Swindon Works under clear signals with a heavily laden west-bound Class 8 loose-coupled freight. (N.L.Browne)

129) In this picture we have a splendid panoramic view of the trackwork to the west of Swindon station with a host of lower quadrant signals to be seen. On 25th April 1954 one of the powerful Churchward GWR 4700 Class 2-8-0's, No 4707 (81A Old Oak Common) finds employment at the head of a Railway Correspondence and Travel Society special which is on its way back to London. Withdrawn in May 1964, No 4707 was scrapped at King's, Norwich. (N.L.Browne)

130) Smoke and steam from the front end of GWR *Castle* Class 4-6-0 No 5038 *Morlais Castle*, of 81A Old Oak Common, swirl around in the wind at Swindon station as the fireman prepares to provide refreshment for his charge on 12th August 1956 which is heading an up express. Constructed in June 1935, *Morlais Castle* spent its last few years of service from the depots at 84G Shrewsbury, 81F Oxford and 81D Reading prior to withdrawal in September 1963. (N.L.Browne)

131) The presence of this permanent way train and a crane suggests to us that 21st October 1962 may have been a Sunday for the access to and from Swindon station would have been somewhat restricted. In charge of the p.w. train is locally based (82C) GWR 1600 Class 0-6-0PT No 1621 which is only three months away from condemnation despite being introduced into service after nationalisation. It was cut up at Swindon later in the year. (F.Hornby)

132) A 'stranger-in-the-camp' - circa 1961. Having been serviced at the nearby shed LNER B1 Class 4-6-0 No 61169, from 41A Sheffield (Darnall), prepares itself for the short run to the station to take the Sunday's Only Swindon to Sheffield express via Oxford. This engine would have been a nice 'cop' for spotters being present so deep into Western Region territory. At the end of 1962, No 61169 moved on to 41F Mexborough. (Tim Farebrother)

133) Enthusiasts 'trespass' on the railway in the left of the frame where we can just make out the outline of Swindon station. Rows of lower quadrant signal posts stand like sentinels as GWR *Hall* Class 4-6-0 No 4932 *Hatherton Hall*, allocated to 83B Taunton, heads westwards on a cold looking and overcast 23rd February 1958. *Hatherton Hall* remained at Taunton shed until October 1964 when it was briefly based at 87A Neath and 86E Severn Tunnel Junction. (F.Hornby)

134) As a direct contrast to the previous photograph it is warm and sunny on 8th May 1955 as GWR *Castle* Class 4-6-0 No 7002 *Devizes Castle* (87F Llanelly) clatters over pointwork and reaches a boarded crossing with an express. By January 1957 *Devizes Castle* was working from 87G Carmarthen where it remained until June 1958 when it moved on to 87E Landore. A final move in December 1959 took it to 85A Worcester where it died in March 1964. (B.K.B Green)

135) Taken from the vantage point of a stationery train standing in Swindon the preserved GWR *City* Class 4-4-0 No 3440, *City of Truro* makes a grand entrance as it trundles along on a through road with a Stephenson Locomotive Society special on 1st September 1957. Built in 1903 at Swindon Works to the design of William Dean, *City of Truro* was withdrawn in 1931 and then housed at York Museum. She was restored to a working condition in 1957 (B.K.B.Green)

136) A lone railwayman, hands in pockets, stands in a safe position as GWR *King* Class 4-6-0 No 6002 *King William IV*, an 81A Old Oak Common steed, approaches Swindon station with an express on 8th May 1955. In the distance, standing next to the signalbox, is a GWR 0-6-0PT. During the latter stages of its lengthy career, *King William IV*, equipped with a double chimney in March 1956, served from 83D Laira and 84A Wolverhampton (Stafford Road). (B.K.B.Green)

137) The importance of Swindon as a market town was enhanced in June 1841 when Brunel's London to Bristol line of the Great Western Railway was completed through the town which up until then contained only 2,500 inhabitants, soon to be increased with the coming of the railway. On an unknown day in 1959 GWR 2800 Class 2-8-0 No 3866, from 86J Aberdare and in fine external condition, speeds eastwards with a freight from South Wales. (D.K.Jones)

138) The GWR 14xx and 58xx series of 0-4-2 Tanks were almost identical although the latter were not fitted with push-pull equipment and their pedigree dated back to the days of Armstrong and Dean and proved themselves to be very capable. On 15th March 1960 the sole survivor of the 58xx series, No 5815, from the local shed, is employed on a freight at Swindon station. After withdrawal in April 1961 it was stored at Swindon for over three years. (Tim Farebrother)

139) The original shed at Swindon, coded 82C in BR days, was constructed in 1871 and eventually ended up as a large roundhouse plus another roundhouse/straight shed. In this picture, taken on 21st October 1962, there is a visit by enthusiasts who are occupying one of the roundhouses. Lurking in the left of the frame is a complete stranger, S & D Class 8F 2-8-0 No 53805. Also present is GWR 2251 Class 0-6-0 No 2244 and two Pannier Tanks. (N.L.Browne)

140) Yet another shed visit by enthusiasts. This time the date is 24th September 1961 where we are out in the open in front of the dilapidated depot structure. On view in the sunshine are four locomotives of which three can be positively identified. On the left is WD Class 8F 2-8-0 No 90315, from 84C Banbury, next to which is locally based GWR *Castle* Class 4-6-0 No 5035 *Coity Castle*. On the right is GWR 2800 Class 2-8-0 No 3802 (84B Oxley). (F.Hornby)

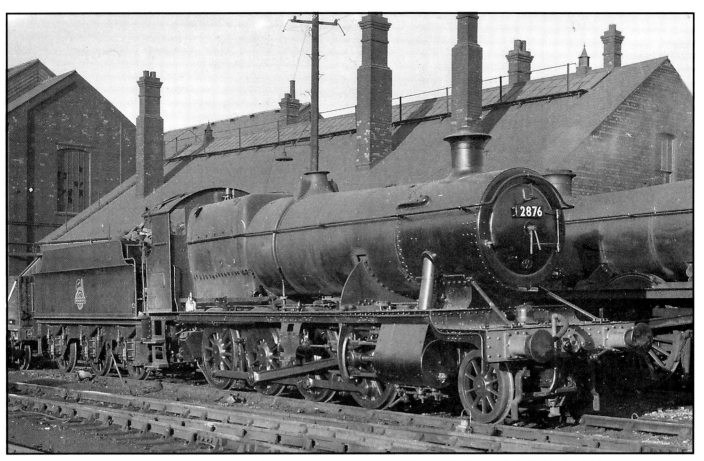

141) Judging by the gleaming coupling rods and freshly painted smokebox GWR 2800 Class 2-8-0 No 2876, of 86J Aberdare, has had a light repair at Swindon as it waits in the shed yard at 82C to be steamed on 12th December 1956. No 2876 was destined to remain as a South Wales based locomotive until withdrawal in January 1965 being transferred from Aberdare to Newport (Ebbw Junction) in August 1963. It was cut up by Birds of Risca, (N.L.Browne)

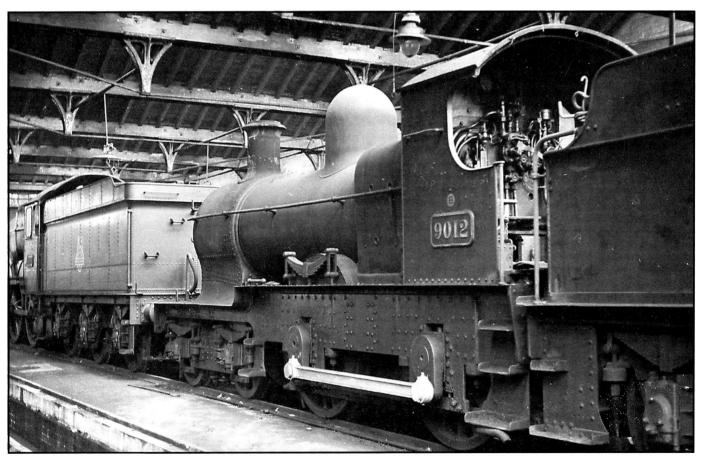

142) All appears silent inside part of the stock shed at Swindon on 24th February 1957. With a GWR *Castle/King* Class 4-6-0 in the left of the frame the focus of attention by the photographer is of former Cambrian Railways 9000 Class 'Dukedog' 4-4-0 No 9012 an inmate of 82C. Built in May 1937 as No 9212 this locomotive has 'Bulldog' frames and a 'Duke' boiler. Although not condemned until July 1957 it is doubtful if it was steamed again. (F.Hornby)

143) A crowded scene outside Swindon shed on a sunny 14th September 1952 where a number of tank engine types and a mogul are gathered. Nearest the camera is GWR 5800 Class 0-4-2T No 5800, withdrawn from 82C in July 1958. Next to No 5800 and fresh from overhaul is GWR 4300 Class 2-6-0 No 5370, from 84E Tyseley. The latter engine remained at 84E until August 1959 being drafted to 87F Llanelly from whence it was condemned in September 1960. (B.K.B.Green)

144) Two ex. works locomotives stand back to back in the yard at Swindon shed on 20th September 1953. Facing us is 4500 Class 2-6-2T No 5535, of 82A Bristol (Bath Road), and BR Class 4 4-6-0 No 75043, allocation not known. No 5535 was taken out of service from 82A in June 1957 whereas No 75043 survived until December 1967 after being based at Bedford, Leicester (Midland), Derby, Walton-on-the-Hill, Aintree and Carnforth sheds. (B.K.B.Green)

145) Released from Swindon Works after overhaul GWR *Hall* Class 4-6-0 No 6941 *Fillongley Hall* has been steamed at Swindon shed and is ready to perform its daily duties on 20th September 1953. For many years during the fifties and early sixties *Fillongley Hall* had a home at 83D Laira (Plymouth). During the last year or so of its life it was allocated to 88L Cardiff East Dock, 83B Taunton and 86G Pontypool Road. The end came in April 1964. (B.K.B.Green)

46) With two GWR 2800 Class 2-8-0's intruding into this picture the centrepiece is of GWR 6100 Class 2-6-2T No 6123, from 81D Reading (minus shedplate). No 6123 is fresh from shops and proudly displays the large 'Lion on Wheel' logo at 82C on an unknown date in 1954. This locomotive, primarily designed for surburban work, later worked from the sheds at 81B Slough and 81F Oxford before being condemned from the latter in April 1962. (D.K.Jones)

147) The BR Class 4 4-6-0's were versatile and popular locomotives and Swindon shed possessed a small number of them, though not No 75001 which is a visitor to 82C on 25th April 1954 a few short years after construction. Allocated to 81F Oxford, No 75001 remained there until March 1963 when it moved to 82E Bristol Barrow Road. In September of this same year it moved on to 83E Yeovil from where it was withdrawn in December 1964. (N.L.Browne)

148) Designed by Collett and first introduced into service in 1934 the GWR 1366 Class of 0-6-0 Pannier Tanks only numbered a total of six of which two, Nos 1369 and 1371, were based at 82C on 16th October 1960 when this picture was taken. Here we see No 1371 in steam by the coal stage a few days prior to withdrawal. It was cut up at Swindon in May 1961. The other locomotive, No 1369, was later saved by the Dart Valley Railway. (F.Hornby)

149) With a somewhat overstocked tender and gleaming front end GWR *Hall* Class 4-6-0 No 5981 *Frensham Hall*, of 84G Shrewsbury, waits to return home after an intermediate overhaul at Swindon Works. It is seen here posing outside the shed structure at 82C on 6th November 1955. Surviving in revenue earning service until September 1962, *Frensham Hall* also served from the sheds at 82F Weymouth, 83A Newton Abbot and 87A Neath. (N.L.Browne)

150) During the mid to late fifties Swindon shed had four of the GWR 5800 series of 0-4-2 Tanks on its books, these being Nos 5800/2/4/5. On 12th August 1956 No 5805 is employed as a shed pilot and is noted at rest beneath the elevated track to the coaling plant which is occupied by a rake of coal wagons. On this date the end was on the horizon for No 5805 with withdrawal looming in March 1958. It was cut up shortly afterwards. (N.L.Browne)

151) At its height Swindon shed was a cosmopolitan place and a visit there often produced a surprise of some sort. In this case the 'surprise' is LNER B1 Class 4-6-0 No 61181, from 41A Sheffield (Darnall), on 14th October 1951. Keeping No 61181 company is an unidentified BR Standard locomotive and an ex.works GWR 4500 Class 2-6-2T No 4585 native to 82C. The host of smoke vents in the background help to complete this picture. (A.J.Pike)

152) Like Eastleigh, Swindon Works started overhauling 'foreign' locomotives from other regions as the steam native to the Western Region began to disappear in droves. In this shot we see LMS Class 4 2-6-0 No 43047 (9F Heaton Mersey) keeping company with GWR *Grange* Class 4-6-0 No 6866 *Morfa Grange* (2A Tyseley) in front of the shed at 82C on 26th July 1964. No 43047 ended its days off the beaten track at the outpost of 12D Workington. (F.Hornby)

153) The late autumn shadows are cast across the yard at 82C on 16th November 1958 as yet another LNER Bl Class 4-6-0 is captured on film. No 61271, from 2F Woodford Halse and in filthy external condition, arrived at Swindon with an express from York which it worked on from Woodford. No 61271 remained on the books at Woodford Halse until becoming another statistic in the mass withdrawals of September 1962. (F.Hornby)

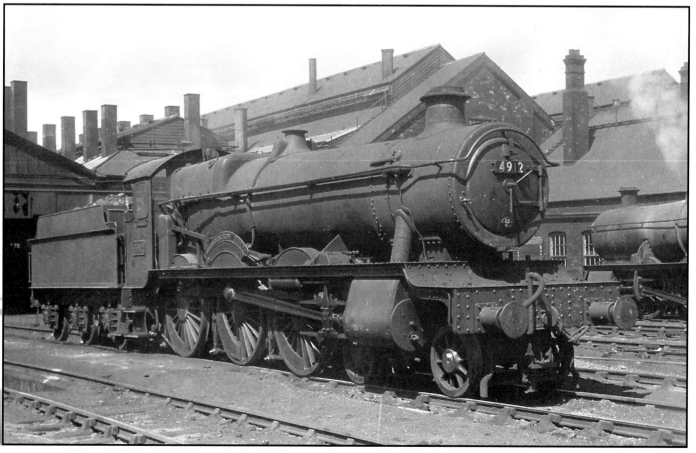

154) With its smaller capacity tender GWR *Hall* Class 4-6-0 No 4912 *Berrington Hall*, a local steed, looks similar in appearance to a GWR *Saint* Class 4-6-0, as it rests in the yard at 82C during the fifties. Transferred during this decade to the Wolverhampton area, *Berrington Hall* served at both Stafford Road and Oxley sheds prior to condemnation in August 1962. Swindon shed closed its doors to steam on 2nd November 1964. (D.K.Jones)

155) We reach the final venue in this album, that of the mighty Swindon Works, which once covered 155 acres, employed almost 6,000 people and at one time constructed some 100 steam locomotives and repaired around a 1,000 annually. As well as having regular open days steam specials also arrived filled with enthusiasts as is the case with the train hauled by GWR 2800 Class 2-8-0 No 3863 seen in the yard on 15th August 1965. (D. Webster)

156) A dull and cloudy day outside Swindon Works on 25th April 1954 as GWR 1366 Class 0-6-0PT No 1366 sets off with a three-coach special to Highworth. In the right of the frame, awaiting attention inside the Works, is a GWR 1400 Class 0-4-2T and a GWR 5700 Class 0-6-0PT No 9730. The locomotive hauling the Railway Correspondence and Travel Society train was the second member of the class to be withdrawn, from 83B Taunton in January 1961. (Peter Hay)

157) Locomotives from all over the Western Region were despatched to Swindon at some time or another for either an overhaul or for scrapping. Unfortunately for this particular engine it is the latter reason. Isolated and never to move a wheel in action again GWR 4200 Class 2-8-0T No 4274 looks a lonely sight at Swindon Works on 12th August 1962 two months after withdrawal from 88H Tondu. It was scrapped at Swindon in October 1962. (N.L.Browne)

158) In direct contrast to the sad sight in the previous picture GWR *Modified Hall.* Class 4-6-0 No 6985 *Parwick Hall* (85B Gloucester - Horton Road) is in steam on 12th February 1956. The reason for the 'live' visit of No 6985 was to take advantage of the turntable facility at Swindon Works whilst the shed ones were out of action. To the left of *Parwick Hall* is an ex.works locomotive. Observe the immense water tower in the background. (N.L.Browne)

159) The following sequence of four photographs are devoted to the very 'hub' of Swindon Works - The Repair Shop. In the first print we espy a group of visitors, including a lady (a rare event to say the least). The main subject is of 86C Cardiff (Canton) based BR *Britannia* Class 4-6-2 No 70024 *Vulcan* stripped to the bare bones for a major overhaul on a Sunday in 1960. Note the heavy lifting gantry in this picture. (Tim Farebrother)

160) Standing amidst a number of driving wheels is an almost completed locomotive following its overhaul inside 'A' shop. With its paintwork gleaming GWR 6100 Class 2-6-2T No 6126, from 81E Didcot, poses for the camera. To the right of No 6126 is the tenderless sight of GWR *Castle* Class 4-6-0 No 5063 *Earl Baldwin*, of 84A Stafford Road (Wolverhampton), which is also nearing completion after an overhaul at the Works on 12th August 1962. (N.L.Browne)

161) Despite the fact that the former Great Western sheds in the West Midlands became the property of the London Midland Region authorities in 1962/63, their occupants continued to be sent to Swindon Works for light and heavy repairs. Minus the front bogies, GWR *Castle* Class 4-6-0 No 7019 *Fowey Castle*, from 2B Oxley, stands near to a *Western* Diesel-Hydraulic No D1065 *Western Consort* on 22nd March 1964. (N.L.Browne)

162) Another locomotive nearing completion is GWR 2800 Class 2-8-0 No 2895, allocated to 86E Severn Tunnel Junction, which may well have been undertaking its last major overhaul. Fitted with the 'luxury' of a side-window cab, No 2895, seen at Swindon Works on 12th August 1962, later served from the sheds at 88L Cardiff East Dock, 88J Aberdare and 86B Newport (Ebbw Junction) prior to condemnation from the latter in April 1965. (N.L.Browne)

163) In steam at Swindon Works whilst utilising the turntable on 12th February 1956 is a work-stained GWR 7200 Class 2-8-2T No 7241, from 86C Cardiff (Canton). The fifty-four members of this heavy freight class were not affected by withdrawals until December 1962, a rare feat by this date in time. However, the picture was to change rapidly and by the end of 1964 there were only ten working examples left in stock, Nos 7201/5/10/22/32/44/48/49/52/53. (N.L.Browne)

164) Hawksworth's thirty members of the *County* Class of 1945-47 were the ultimate two cylinder 4-6-0's of the Great Western Railway and were most unusual in the fact that they had straight instead of curved nameplates. Although appearing with single chimneys, all were later modified with double ones. On 31st October 1954, No 1026 *County of Salop* looks immaculate as it awaits steaming and the return to its home at 84G Shrewsbury. (N.L.Browne)

165) A once common sight outside Swindon Works were row upon row of steam engines waiting to be reunited with their tenders. Three such locomotives are on view on 12th February 1956. In the centre of the frame is GWR *Castle* Class 4-6-0 No 5014 *Goodrich Castle* (81A Old Oak Common) which allows us a rare insight of the footplate. *Goodrich Castle*, built in June 1932, was withdrawn from 2A Tyseley in February 1965 and scrapped shortly after. (N.L.Brown)

166) Swindon Works was responsible for constructing many of the BR Class 9F 2-10-0's which of course culminated with No 92220 *Evening Star* being the last steam locomotive to be built by British Railways. On 23rd February 1958 a brand new example, No 92178, equipped with a double chimney, awaits the arrival of its tender. Allocated to 34E New England, No 92178 had a very short life being condemned from 41J Langwith Junction in October 1965. (N.L.Browne)

167) With the familiar sight of rows of steam engines disappearing into the distance, the final member, of the robust and reliable GWR *Grange* Class 4-6-0's, No 6879 *Overton Grange*, from 84E Tyseley, stands steamless and minus tender in the Works yard at Swindon on 21st October 1962 near to an unidentified boiler. *Overton Grange*, once of 83D Laira (Plymouth), 83F Truro, 83E St.Blazey and 84F Stourbridge survived until October 1965. (F.Hornby)

168) GWR *Castle* Class 4-6-0 No 7013 *Bristol Castle*, built in 1948, inside 'A' shop at Swindon Works on 16th February 1952. This locomotive was at the centre of controversy at the time, having three days previously worked the funeral train of King George VI from Paddington to Windsor under the 'assumed' guise of No 4082 *Windsor Castle*. The square-topped inside cylinder cover is an indication that this is a 7000 series of *Castle*. (A.N.H.Glover)

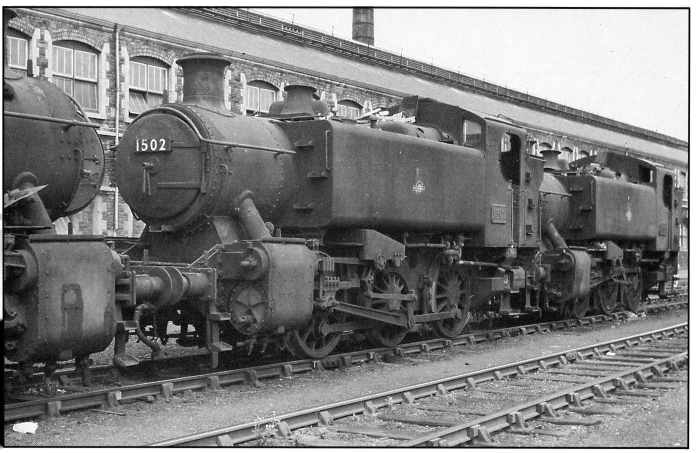

69) A trio of Hawksworth inspired GWR 1500 Class 0-6-0 Pannier Tanks are parked outside the Swindon factory on 28th May 1961. Facing us are Nos 1502, once of 81E Didcot and 1504, from 81A Old Oak Common. No 1502, withdrawn in January 1961, was destined to be sold to the Coal Board where it was employed until late in 1970. No 1504 is in for overhaul and was not taken out of revenue earning service from Old Oak until May 1963. (F.Hornby)

70) An unidentified member of the 86C Cardiff (Canton) fleet of BR *Britannia* Class 4-6-2's nestles up to the tenderless form of BR Class 9F 2-10-0 No 92079, the 'Lickey Banker' based at 85F Bromsgrove, as it awaits an overhaul at Swindon on 26th July 1959. No 92079 remained on 'The Lickey' until October 1963 when it was drafted away to Merseyside, to 8H Birkenhead, where it worked heavy and medium freights until November 1967. (F.Hornby)

171) Unlike Crewe, Doncaster and Eastleigh, Swindon had masses of space for the storage and disposal of steam locomotives until it too was overwhelmed by mass withdrawals. In this picture, taken on 24th May 1959, endless rows of doomed engines await their inevitable fate, including two GWR 1400 Class 0-4-2 Tanks Nos 1457 and 1467, both withdrawn in April 1959 from 85D Kidderminster and 85B Gloucester (Horton Road) respectively. (N.E.Preedy)

172) GWR 4700 Class 2-8-0 No 4706, withdrawn from 81A Old Oak Common in February 1964, rots away at Swindon Dump on 26th April 1964. Sadly not one of these powerful Churchward engines nine in total, was ever preserved. No 4706, introduced in March 1923, spent many years on fast freight services between London and Bristol and was occasionally utilised for passenger traffic in its latter years. It was cut up not long after this photo was taken. (Tim Farebrother)

173) With rows of mineral wagons fore and aft this rear-end view of GWR 2021 Class 0-6-0PT No 2122 clearly shows the vacuum brake pipes, lamp brackets, grab rails and hooks for a shunter's pole - modellers please note! On this grey and drab looking day in June 1953, No 2122 is parked in the yard at Swindon Works' dreaded 'C' shop. Soon it will be called by the executioner for a date with the cutter's torch and oblivion. (B.K.B.Green)

74) The 4200 series of the GWR 4200 Class 2-8-0 Tanks were designed by Churchward and first came into service in 1910 and most were employed from depots in South Wales on heavy freight trains. The pioneer member of the class, No 4200, condemned from 86A Newport (Ebbw Junction) in March 1959, stands in a line-up at Swindon Dump on 26th July 1959. Despite being near to 'C' shop it was eventually scrapped at Wards, Briton Ferry. (N.L.Browne)

175) From the humblest tank engine to the mightiest of 4-6-0's nothing was spared in this scrapyard of scrapyards. On 12th August 1962 a trio of tenderless tender locomotives await their grim fate in silence. Nearest the camera, built at Swindon Works in March 1928, GWR *King* Class 4-6-0 No 6008 *King James 11* is ready to die at its birthplace. It had been withdrawn from 84A Wolverhampton (Stafford Road) in June 1962. (N.L.Browne)

176) This picture of a trio of tank engines at Swindon scrapyard brings to an end this album of memories of four once great railway centres. In the left of the frame is GWR 4200 Class 2-8-0T No 4203, withdrawn in January 1961 from 86A Newport (Ebbw Junction) seen on 28th May 1961. In the centre of the photograph is GWR 5100 Class 2-6-2T No 5176, again withdrawn in January 1961, from 84F Stourbridge, behind which is a 9400 Class 0-6-0PT. (N.L.Browne)